THE FREQUENT TRAVELER'S GUIDE TO PACKING

50 PACKING HACKS TO TRAVEL LIGHT, MAXIMIZE SPACE, AND SIMPLIFY STRESS-FREE TRAVEL

ALEX WYLER

First published in 2024 by Alex Wyler of AW World Books of Jeff Tucker Homesteading Press in the United Kingdom.

ISBN: 9781068575525

A CIP catalogue record for this book is available
from the British Library.

Typeset by AW World Books of
Jeff Tucker Homesteading Press.

Cover art and design by AW World Books of
Jeff Tucker Homesteading Press.

Dedicated to all of the travelers,
especially those who know and trust in
the fun to be had
at every single leg of the journey.

Contents

Introduction

ELCOME TO *THE FREQUENT TRAVELER'S Guide to Packing*, your ultimate companion for stress-free, organized, and efficient travel. I'm so thrilled you've picked up this book, because, whether you're a seasoned jet-setter or someone looking to sstreamline their travel routine, this book is here to make your journeys easier, lighter, and more enjoyable.

I was inspired to write this book after seeing one of my friends—a frequent traveler for business and professional seminars and events—commenting on a social media post that discussed traveling lighter. I had the immediate epiphany that she would really benefit from one go-to resource that detailed a number of high-value, time-saving, organization-friendly hacks, because, reading her comments, she clearly didn't have anything like it in one place. As a frequent traveler myself, I quickly got to work compiling all of my favorite, most commonly used *pack hacks*, and here we are!

If you've ever stood over a suitcase, wrestling with zippers and wondering why it feels impossible to pack everything you need, let me tell you: there is a better way (and not just one but many). Travel is supposed to be exciting, but all too often the process of packing and navigating the actual *travel* part can feel like an obstacle. How do you make sure you're prepared without overpacking? How do you avoid costly mistakes like overweight luggage fees or forgotten essentials? How do you make the most of your precious suitcase space while keeping your favorite items intact and accessible? And how do you pack things that give you the comfort of being at home while away from home?

This book is packed (pun intended!) with clever tips, time-tested tricks, and creative hacks to solve many of the problems regular travelers experience with every trip. It's designed to help you:

- Travel light without feeling like you've left half your essentials behind;
- Maximize space so you can fit what you need and avoid bulky, overstuffed bags; and
- Simplify your packing routine to save time and reduce pre-trip stress.

In addition, every hack has been detailed in a concise, time-efficient way, so that you can reference hacks at a glance and not spend too much of your precious time reading and re-reading, because I know better than most: you'd rather be off trotting the globe!

Why Packing Smart Matters

Packing isn't just about fitting things into a bag; it sets the tone for your entire trip. A well-packed suitcase means fewer worries, smoother transitions, and more time to focus on the experience itself—which is what it's actually all about. So, by mastering the art of packing, traveling light, and giving yourself the nurture and comforts you really enjoy, you'll be in an amazing position to enjoy far more freedom and flexibility during your travels.

For frequent travelers, this can honestly change the game. When you're on the road—or in the air—even small improvements can make a huge difference. A leak-proof toiletries hack, a method for keeping your clothes fresh, or a quick trick to find lost luggage could save you time, money, and unnecessary frustration.

When I gave the proof copy of this book to the friend who inspired this entire project, she couldn't believe how quickly the hacks transformed her packing. Even though she already considered herself a smart packer, she learned some new tips and tricks that made a huge difference, because it really doesn't matter how seasoned you are at anything: you don't know what you don't know.

This book isn't about reinventing the wheel. Instead, it's more about giving you simple, practical solutions that you can apply immediately. They've been written in a super simple, info-at-a-glance way so that you can approach this whole time-saving approach without laboring over a book every time you want to find a new method (not my style and somewhat pointless when we're looking to streamline things). These hacks are designed to work for a variety of travelers—whether you're heading out for a weekend getaway, a business trip, or a longer adventure. Wherever you want to go and however you want to get there and for however long, I've written this book with the goal of you finding something here that makes you think, "Wow. From now on, I'm doing *that* every single time I travel!"

How to Use This Book

In mind of making this guide as helpful as possible, I've structured it to provide easy reference. Each short chapter focuses on a specific aspect of packing, from choosing the right bag to maximizing space and staying organized on the go. You'll find plenty of actionable tips, and for even more convenience, I've created a type of symbol system to highlight the key benefits of each hack:

- ⊠ Space-Saving Hacks to help you pack smarter.
- ⌧ Time-Saving Hacks to streamline your routine.
- $ Money-Saving Hacks to keep your budget intact.
- ✈ Convenience Hacks to make your trip stress-free.
- # Organizational Hacks to keep everything tidy and accessible.

At the back of the book, you'll find a Quick Reference Index that lets you easily locate all the hacks within a specific category (and although I genuinely love all of this guide, I have to say: this is my favorite part). Whether you're short on time or just want to jump straight to the hacks that matter most to you, this index-of-sorts will make finding what you need a breeze.

In addition, you'll find a section that gives you an easy-to-reference list of hacks that would be great for different groups or purposes, such as Best For Families and Best For Business Travelers. I hope you'll find a lot of value here and be able to skip to the parts you need most.

A Final Word Before We Begin

Packing really doesn't have to be a chore. It doesn't need to be stressful. And it doesn't need to be a constant game of *I can take this or that*. With a few little gems of knowledge and a handful of clever tricks, it can become part of the adventure (because not much compares to the satisfaction of knowing you can get up and go at the drop of a (sun)hat without constantly throwing yourself into a battle of baggage wars).

This guide is here to inspire and empower you to take control of your packing routine, so you can focus on what really matters to you: the joy of travel and all that awaits when you get to your next destination.

Of course, as with all of the hacks detailed in this book, you may already know and regularly make use of some of them, but you might also just find a new favorite here that will change how you travel forever, and that is not only my hope but has been the overriding goal I held when writing every chapter.

So, grab your bags, and let's get started. Your next trip is going to be your smoothest one yet.

—ALEX WYLER

Chapter 1:
The Right Bag

ALTHOUGH I WOULD LOVE TO jump straight into the different hacks and tips I have for you, I would be a poor *packing guide* if I neglected to briefly touch on the importance of choosing the right bags for travel. Of course, if you're a seasoned traveler and you have already weighed the pros and cons of suitcase versus duffel, by all means, skip to the next chapter. But if you're open to considering an alternative or you really need help choosing, this is for you.

Your ability to pack smart isn't necessarily dictated by your chosen bag, but it definitely changes the course of where you put things and how you put them there. Your suitcase, backpack, or duffel is more than just a container for your belongings—without wanting to sound overly dramatic, it really is the foundation of your entire travel experience. A well-chosen bag can make navigating airports, train stations, and city streets a breeze, while the wrong bag can leave you frustrated, uncomfortable, or unprepared—and, worse still, dreading the next airport or travel experience.

Many travelers fall into the trap of using whatever bag they have to hand, without really giving much thought to whether it's actually suited to their trip. Maybe it's too big, leaving you tempted to overpack, or maybe it's too small, forcing you to leave essentials behind (which can mean missing home and which ultimately steals some of the joy of traveling). A poorly designed bag can also make it harder to stay organized, leading to frantic digging through your things when you need something in a hurry.

In this chapter, we'll take a quick look at how to choose the perfect bag for your trip (and, spoiler alert, how it looks really doesn't and shouldn't come into it) and share a few hacks to make the selection process even easier.

Types of Bags

Different trips call for different types of luggage, but there are some common options that align best with certain types of trips:

1. **Carry-Ons**

    Carry-ons tend to be a go-to option for travelers due to their key advantages: they allow you to reduce time spent at the airport (we all know checking luggage can be time-consuming and costly) and being able to keep everything you need close by and accessible during a flight. Look for a carry-on that includes compartments for toiletries, electronics, and a few changes of clothes. It's important to look for one that meets airline size requirements, but still be sure to do your research when booking flights: some airlines have been known to be a little sneaky and deviate from the normal sizing specifications, meaning you'll unexpectedly need to check or pay for your carry-on. Never fun!

2. **Backpacks**

    Backpacks are a top choice for travelers who like to keep their travel hands-free. With the flexibility and mobility they offer, they are the ideal choice for navigating busy streets or uneven terrain, and allow you to keep your essentials close without the hassle of carrying a separate bag. When choosing the perfect backpack, I would recommend looking for one with padded straps and different compartments so that you can keep items like electronics, toiletries, and clothing well-organized. However, it has to be said: not all backpacks are created equal— some can be deceptively low on space or might not offer the structure needed for longer trips. Most importantly, your back and shoulders can become strained if you overpack and carry too much weight. It's therefore super important to choose a lightweight, ergonomic design so that you can be comfortable during your travels, whether long or short.

3. **Duffel Bags**

If you like the idea of a laid-back travel style, a well-designed duffel bag might just be your go-to. Duffels provide a casual, flexible packing option, making them perfect for road trips, overnight stays, or minimalist travelers. Their lightweight design, coupled with soft, flexible material, means they can fit easily into car trunks or tight spaces. It's common for duffels to now include wheels for that additional convenience, meaning luggage can be rolled with the flexibility of a traditional duffel. That being said, however, duffels tend to be without compartments, meaning keeping things organized can be tricky at best. In addition, carrying a heavy duffel over long distances can be strenuous and frustrating.

4. **Checked Luggage**

For those travelers planning longer trips or carrying bulkier items, checked luggage is the obvious choice. In these situations, larger suitcases are the perfect option for packing winter coats, boots, or even souvenirs you might want to have the option of bringing home. If checked luggage feels aligned, look for something lightweight, with strong, sturdy wheels, and an all-important secure locking mechanism to protect your belongings. Although checked luggage frees you from carrying heavy bags through the airport, they do, however, present a few downsides: the risk of lost luggage, longer waits at baggage claim and the potential for additional fees to provide a nasty surprise the day of travel.

Choosing the Best Bag for Your Trip

When deciding on the type of bag for you and your trip, consider these key factors at a glance:

- **Trip Length:** A weekend getaway often means you'll need far less than a two-week vacation. Carry-ons or backpacks tend to be the best option for short trips, whereas longer journeys might mean a suitcase is the go-to option.
- **Travel Style:** Business travelers might see the need to opt for a sleeker carry-on with compartments for electronics, whereas leisure travelers might prefer something offering a greater degree of versatility.
- **Destination:** A city trip often calls for wheels for smooth sidewalks, whereas a more rugged destination might mean a backpack with strong straps is the better option.

Essentially, the choice of which bag to opt for might be influenced by a number of factors. Considering all of the above can be really helpful in deciding on the right choice for your needs on a trip-by-trip basis.

Features to Look For

When making your choice, the very best travel bags combine practicality and convenience and will offer *the best of all worlds*. However, at times, there are trade-offs that need to be taken into account and balanced. Consider prioritizing as follows:

- **Lightweight Durability:** Seek out bags made with materials like polycarbonate or nylon. These won't add unnecessary weight, and can also tolerate wear and tear.

- **Organizational Compartments:** Pockets and dividers provide so much flexibility with packing, and make it easier to separate clothing, toiletries, and electronics.
- **Spinner Wheels:** Four wheels with 360-degree rotation make navigating crowded airports or narrow train aisles effortless. A little extra expense may be incurred when buying something like this, but the additional ease is well worth it.
- **TSA-Friendly Features:** Bags with easily accessible laptop compartments or locks that are approved by airport security standards can make all the difference when moving through security and being time-efficient.

Tips for Bag Selection

Choosing the right bag is easier when you know these insider tips:

- **Test Before You Buy:** Pack your bag with a mock trip's worth of items to ensure it's the right size and layout for your needs. If it isn't, most stores and online retailers provide refunds within a certain period of time, so if it isn't going to do the job, simply return it.
- **Look for USB Ports:** A backpack with a built-in USB port allows you to charge your devices on the go. Simply connect a power bank inside, and you're set. This can give so much peace of mind when heading to airports, where having charged devices ready to power on is often required for security checks.
- **Consider Expandability:** If you want to have the option to go shopping or pick up souvenirs, a bag with expandable sections will provide flexibility without the need to buy a second suitcase or bag. Again, additional expense might save a lot more money in the long-run.

At-a-Glance Pros and Cons

Carry-Ons

Benefits:

- *Easy to keep close, reducing the risk of lost luggage.*
- *Avoid any unexpected checked luggage fees.*
- *Allows for a faster airport experience—no waiting to check baggage in or at baggage claim.*
- *The compact size forces you to pack light.*
- *Fits in overhead bins or under the seat on most airlines.*

Drawbacks:

- *Limited space might mean having to compromise on essentials for longer trips.*
- *Strict airline size and weight restrictions can mean some airlines require carry-on to be checked and/or paid for.*
- *Can be difficult to pack bulkier items, such as winter jackets or boots.*
- *May become heavy to lift into overhead storage compartments.*

Backpacks

Benefits:

- *Allows for hands-free travel and therefore improved mobility.*
- *Great for active trips or destinations where terrain might be uneven.*
- *Usually offering multiple compartments, therefore facilitating easy organization.*
- *Lightweight and flexible for short or adventurous trips.*
- *Often meets carry-on size requirements.*

Drawbacks:
- Can strain your shoulders or back if overpacked or heavy.
- Limited capacity when compared with suitcases.
- Not the most ideal when it comes to protecting delicate or structured items.
- Might feel or look less professional when traveling for business.

Duffel Bags

Benefits:
- Lightweight and easy to carry.
- Flexible shape fits easily into car trunks or odd spaces.
- Casual and versatile for different trip types.
- Available in wheeled options for easier transport.

Drawbacks:
- Somewhat limited when it comes to organizational compartments.
- Can strain your shoulders if carried for long distances.
- The lack of structure makes it more difficult to pack in the most efficient way.
- Far from ideal when it comes to more fragile items or professional settings.

Checked Luggage

Benefits:
- Offers the most space for extended trips.
- Ideal for packing bulky or specialty items, such as coats, boots, or sportswear.

- *Allows for liquids over TSA limits to be carried and taken abroad.*
- *Durable designs are better able to protect fragile or more valuable items.*

Drawbacks:
- *There is a risk of lost or delayed luggage.*
- *Longer wait times at baggage check-in and/or baggage claim.*
- *Checked luggage fees can really add up and reduce budgets allocated for destination spending.*
- *The temptation to overpack could result in overweight fees.*

Choosing the right bag requires far more thought than simply picking a container for your belongings—after all, your bag is your travel companion that can quite literally take the weight and make the days and steps in the journey so much easier. With all of this in mind, you'll want to take time when it comes to choosing the right one that suits your trip, your style, your needs, and any tendencies you have, i.e. shopping for souvenirs. With the right foundation, packing becomes easier, and your travels become infinitely smoother.

Now, are you ready to pack smart? Let's move on to the essentials you'll need to fill your bag and the best ways to organize them.

Chapter 2:
Packing Hacks for Every Trip

PACKING SMART IS A UNIVERSAL skill, no matter where you're headed. In this chapter, you'll find a list of at-a-glance, versatile hacks that will work for any type of traveler, trip, destination, or duration. These tips have all been considered and detailed here in mind of helping to save you that much-needed space, keep you organized, and simplify your travel routine.

Hack 1: Don't Skip Packing Cubes

☒ Space-Saving | # Organizational

Packing cubes are a must when you're looking to optimize space and stay organized. They can be used to sort your items by category—bulky items in larger cubes, and smaller items, such as socks and underwear, in smaller ones. Compression cubes are especially effective for saving space, and extras can separate clean and dirty clothes.

Hack 2: Roll Clothes Instead of Folding

☒ Space-Saving | ☒ Time-Saving

Rolling clothes can save up to 25% more space than folding, and also helps in the fight against travel-induced wrinkles. As most of us don't take travel irons with us (especially considering our want and need to travel light), focus on rolling soft, wrinkle-resistant fabrics, like T-shirts and leggings. This technique also makes the use of packing cubes or suitcase corners that much more efficient.

Hack 3: Pack Complete Outfits Instead of Random Items

\# Organizational | ☒ Time-Saving

It's super common to pack items that ultimately don't get used or worn. Avoid this by planning your outfits in advance. One recommendation would be to try on every outfit, take a picture, and document it for reference while on your travels so you can remember what you planned to wear and when. Roll each outfit together, including socks and accessories, to save time getting dressed and ensure everything you take with you serves a purpose.

Hack 4: Pack Clothes for Multiple Occasions

☒ Space-Saving | ✈ Convenience

Maximize your wardrobe's versatility by choosing items that can transition between activities, times of day, and purposes. A blouse or button-down can go from sightseeing during the day to dinner at night, while athletic wear could double as loungewear. This reduces the need to pack extra outfits while ensuring you're prepared for any situation and comfortable in all settings.

Hack 5: Use the 1-2-3-4-5-6 Rule for Clothes

☒ Space-Saving | ☒ Time-Saving | $ Money-Saving

Pack one hat, two pairs of shoes, three bottoms, four tops, five pairs of socks, and six pairs of underwear. This simple formula can cover up to two weeks of travel (assuming you're wearing underwear when you travel!). Adjust the numbers based on your destination, but this hack provides a great starting point for packing light.

Hack 6: Spray Cotton Pads with Perfume

✈ Convenience | ⊠ Space-Saving

Keep your clothes smelling fresh by spraying a few cotton pads with your favorite perfume or cologne, and tucking them into your suitcase. Everything will smell nice and fresh, and you won't need to worry about carrying bulky bottles.

Hack 7: Pack Multi-Use Items

⊠ Space-Saving | $ Money-Saving | ✈ Convenience

Choose clothing and accessories that can be worn for multiple days or for different purposes. This will allow you to reduce the number of items you pack. As examples, a sarong can double as a towel or blanket, while zip-off pants can transition between casual wear and hiking gear. Prioritize items that offer more than one function to save space and weight. When you do this, you can easily double the number of outfits you have.

Hack 8: Layer Clothes Instead of Packing Bulky Items

⊠ Space-Saving | $ Money-Saving

Rather than packing a bulky sweater, you could opt for a layering system: start with a base layer, add a long-sleeve shirt, and finish with a lightweight, packable jacket. This method provides both warmth and flexibility while also maximizing your bag's real estate and packing space.

These hacks provide a great foundation for packing smarter. By combining thoughtful planning with a few clever tricks, you'll be ready to pack for any trip with ease.

In the next chapter, we'll look at the challenge of maximizing space in your bag without leaving anything behind.

Chapter 3:
Space-Saving Hacks

WHEN SPACE IS ONE OF your most important considerations, every inch of your bag counts. Whether you're traveling with a carry-on for a weekend getaway or trying to pack light for a month-long adventure, the challenge of fitting everything in can feel like a game of Tetris. This chapter is here to show you how to win that game every time.

With the right approach, packing doesn't have to mean leaving behind the things that make your trip enjoyable. From clever folding techniques to smart tools like compression bags, these space-saving hacks are designed to make the most of every square inch in your bag. Whether you're packing bulky winter coats or small but important accessories, you'll find solutions to help you fit it all without overstuffing or sacrificing your organization.

Plus, by using these strategies, you'll not only create space for souvenirs or last-minute additions, but you'll also avoid the dreaded overpacking trap—saving time, stress, and even money. Ready to transform the way you pack? Let's dive into these simple but powerful tricks.

Hack 9: Use Vacuum-Seal Bags to Shrink Bulky Items

☒ Space-Saving

Vacuum-seal bags are an absolute game-changer when it comes to reducing the size of bulky clothing, like winter jackets or sweaters. Your items will first need to be packed into the bag and the bag sealed. The air is then removed using a vacuum or hand pump. This technique creates so much more space in your chosen bag or suitcase, but do remember to always check with weight limits—condensing items can lead to overpacking.

Hack 10: *Place Clothes in Your Bag Before Vacuum-Sealing*

☒ Space-Saving | # Organizational

For optimal efficiency, pack your suitcase fully before vacuum-sealing any items. This ensures all available space is used and creates small pockets for toiletries, socks, or jewelry. It's a great way to balance organization with space-saving.

Hack 11: *Layer Clothing Items Inside Coats for Space Efficiency*

☒ Space-Saving | ✈ Convenience

Bulky coats and jackets take up precious room in your suitcase. Use this dead space by layering smaller items, such as scarves, socks, or T-shirts inside the coat. This not only saves space but also keeps the coat's shape during travel.

Hack 12: *Wear Your Bulkiest Clothes on the Plane*

☒ Space-Saving | $ Money-Saving

Save space in your bag by wearing heavier, bulkier items, such as boots, jackets, or sweaters, during your flight. Not only does this free up some of that valuable bag real estate, but it also keeps you warm in what can often be a chilly airport terminal or plane cabin. (And if you do find yourself getting hot, you can always loop big coats or jackets through bag handles to facilitate ease of carrying.)

Hack 13: Wrap Belts Around the Inside of Your Suitcase

☒ Space-Saving

Instead of rolling or folding belts, which can lead to them becoming damaged, wrap them around the edges of your suitcase. This clever little trick not only saves space, but keeps belts flat, preventing creasing and cracking.

Hack 14: Pack Hats Upside Down and Fill Them with Socks

☒ Space-Saving

Avoid the dreaded hat distortion and maintain their shape by packing them upside-down in your suitcase. Fill the crown with socks or other small, soft items to maximize space and achieve the ultimate goal: to protect your hat from being crushed.

Hack 15: Use the Hollow Space Beneath Your Suitcase Lining

☒ Space-Saving

Many suitcases have a removable lining that covers the hollow plastic frame. This hidden space can actually be used to maximize space and store awkward, bulky items, such as flat footwear, like sandals or flip-flops. It not only keeps them safe, but frees up room in the main compartment.

Hack 16: Roll Clothes and Use Packing Organizers

☒ Space-Saving | # Organizational

Combine rolling clothes with packing cubes or compression bags to maximize suitcase space. Rolling minimizes wrinkles and creates a compact shape, while organizers keep everything tidy and easy to find.

The two in combination provide a frequent traveler's dream of saving space and achieving maximum organization.

The space-saving hacks shared in this chapter mean you'll have room for all your essentials and then some. By packing smart, you can avoid overstuffed bags, reduce stress, and even save money on checked luggage fees.

In the next chapter, we'll shift focus to staying organized on the go.

Chapter 4:
Organizational Hacks

STAYING ORGANIZED WHILE TRAVELING ISN'T just about packing—it's about creating a system that keeps your essentials easy to find and your bag or suitcase tidy. These hacks are presented to help you maintain order in your luggage, so you can spend less time rummaging and more time enjoying your trip.

Hack 17: Use Shower Caps to Cover Dirty Shoes
Organizational

Buy an inexpensive pack of shower caps from your local store. One shower cap can then be used to cover the soles of your shoes to keep dirt from transferring to your clothes. It's a simple, lightweight solution that keeps your suitcase clean and organized, and stops you worrying about your clothing being marked.

Hack 18: Hook Earrings Onto Buttons to Keep Pairs Together
Organizational

Avoid losing earrings by threading each pair through the holes of a button. Place the buttons, with their earring companions, into a small pouch or zip bag for extra security. This allows you to keep your jewelry neat and safe, and prevents small pieces from becoming lost in transit. Alternatively...

Hack 19: Use an Exfoliating Mitt to Organize Earrings
Organizational
Thread earrings through the material of an exfoliating mitt to keep them organized and paired. This soft, flexible solution is compact and keeps jewelry safe during travel.

Hack 20: Use Straws to Prevent Necklace Tangling
Organizational
Thread one end of a necklace through a straw and clasp it shut to keep the chain straight. This prevents tangles and saves time when you're getting dressed. For multiple necklaces, use different colored straws to make identification easier. Notably, you might need different-length straws for shorter necklaces and thicker straws when the chain is larger than average.

Hack 21: Store Jewelry in a Weekly Pill Organizer
Organizational
A pill organizer, complete with its individual compartments, is the perfect storage container for small jewelry items, such as rings, earrings, and necklaces. Each piece has its own slot, keeping everything safe and easy to access, with limited space for anything to move around and become tangled. You could take this hack to the next level by actually using the pill organizer's day references to guide what you wear on that particular day!

Hack 22: Cotton Pads in Makeup Palettes to Prevent Breakage

Organizational | $ Money-Saving

Protect fragile makeup palettes by placing cotton pads inside before packing. The soft padding absorbs shocks and prevents powders or eyeshadows from cracking during transit. This lightweight, inexpensive hack ensures your beauty products stay intact, helping to ensure no costly replacements.

Hack 23: Separate Dirty Laundry with Packing Cubes

Organizational | ⊠ Space-Saving

Use an extra packing cube to separate dirty laundry from clean clothes. This allows you to keep your suitcase organized and prevents odors from transferring from used, wet or dirty items, to your clean items. As an additional hack, pre-label cubes with 'dirty' and 'clean' to allow you to identify at a glance what can be worn and what needs washing. Notably, compression cubes are especially handy for reducing the bulk of dirty clothes.

Hack 24: Wrap Bottles in Diapers to Prevent Breakage or Leaks

Organizational | ✈ Convenience | $ Money-Saving

Fragile bottles, such as wine or spirits, can break or leak during travel. Protect them by wrapping one diaper around the bottom and another around the top. The padding reduces the risk of breakage, while the absorbency contains any leaks. This keeps your suitcase safe, clean, and free from stains—avoiding unnecessary expenses for replacing damaged items.

Without question, travel is so much easier when your luggage is organized. These hacks ensure everything has a place, so you can quickly find what you need and avoid any unnecessary stress.

In the next chapter, we'll explore hacks for making travel more convenient and enjoyable.

Chapter 5:
Convenience Hacks

TRAVELING DOESN'T HAVE TO BE a hassle. These convenience hacks are all about making your trips smoother and more enjoyable. From staying prepared to keeping essentials within reach, everything detailed here is done so in mind of helping to ensure stress-free travel at every stage of your journey.

Hack 25: Place an AirTag or Tracker in Your Luggage

✈ Convenience

Lost luggage is a nightmare, but an AirTag or Tile tracker can really save the day. Slip one into your suitcase, and use your smartphone to track it in real-time. For added security, hide the tracker in a discreet pocket or beneath the lining of your bag. Being able to track your bag or suitcase can help to take so much of the guesswork out of the equation in the event of misplaced luggage or bags that have lost their way.

Hack 26: Use Travel Dressing Containers for Liquids

✈ Convenience | ⊠ Space-Saving

Small dressing containers can be repurposed for travel-sized amounts of shampoo, conditioner, or liquid soap. These lightweight, leak-proof containers are easy to clean and perfect for ensuring compliance with TSA regulations.

Hack 27: Petroleum Jelly with Perfume for a Solid Scent

✈ Convenience | $ Money-Saving | ⊠ Space-Saving

Create a portable, spill-proof version of your favorite fragrance by mixing a few sprays of perfume or cologne with a small pot of petroleum jelly. Apply a dab to your wrists or neck for a long-lasting scent. This TSA-friendly hack eliminates the need to carry bulky or breakable bottles and can help ensure that a favorite, potentially expensive fragrance isn't lost or, worse yet, confiscated at security.

Hack 28: Trim Your Body Care Routine with Multi-Purpose Products

✈ Convenience | ⊠ Space-Saving

Simplify your toiletry bag by swapping out single-purpose products for multi-functional ones. Shampoo bars that double as body wash, lotion sticks, or waterless cleansers are lightweight, spill-proof, and TSA-compliant. These can be packed in a compact toiletry case to keep everything neat and travel-ready.

Hack 29: Hang Keys or Balance a Coin on Door Handles for Security

✈ Convenience

Create a simple security system that instills peace of mind by hanging keys or balancing a coin on the handle of your hotel or Airbnb door. If the door is opened unexpectedly, the sound of a falling coin or falling keys will alert you. This is an easy, simple and cost-effective way of helping you to feel safe while traveling.

Hack 30: Clip Carabiners to Your Bag for Extra Storage

✈ Convenience | ⊠ Space-Saving

Carabiners can be attached to your backpack or suitcase so that items like a water bottle, jacket, or sandals can be hung. This keeps essentials within reach while also freeing up that high-value space inside your bag. Carabiners are lightweight and perfect for any on-the-go adjustments that might need to be made.

Hack 31: Layer Dryer Sheets in Your Luggage for Fresh Clothes

✈ Convenience

Keep your clothes smelling fresh throughout your trip by placing dryer sheets between layers of clothing. And, as a bonus: you can also use the sheets to freshen up shoes or hotel drawers.

Hack 32: Use Sectioned Tupperware for Snacks or Meals

✈ Convenience | $ Money-Saving | ⊠ Space-Saving

Pack snacks or prepared meals in compact, sectioned Tupperware boxes. Not only will these help to prevent spills and keep food fresh, but they will also save you from purchasing expensive or otherwise overpriced meals and snacks at airports and other outlets. Look for lightweight, stackable designs for added convenience.

Hack 33: Use a Skipping Rope as a Makeshift Clothesline

✈ Convenience

A skipping rope can double as a clothesline when tied around furniture or radiators. To use it, fold the rope in half and twist the two strands together. This creates a secure hold for your clothes—simply tuck the fabric into the twists to hang and dry. Lightweight and multi-functional, this hack is perfect for drying hand-washed clothes on longer trips.

Hack 34: Bring Dish Soap and a Sponge for Cleaning
✈ Convenience

Although you undoubtedly won't want to spend any length of time on your trip cleaning, packing a small, travel-sized tube of dish soap and a sponge can be a lifesaver for cleaning surfaces, dishes, or containers should you find yourself in less-than-pristine accommodations. Pre-cut the sponge into smaller pieces to save space, or opt for soap-infused sponges for added convenience.

With these convenience hacks, your travels can be smoother and more enjoyable. By staying prepared and thinking creatively, you'll find it easier to adapt to unexpected situations and make the most of your trip.

Up next: hacks to save time and maximize efficiency.

Chapter 6:
Time-Saving Hacks

TIME IS ONE OF THE most valuable resources when traveling (and in life in general!) As such, these hacks are provided to help you make the most of every second of your trip, however long that may be. Whether you're preparing for your trip or managing your belongings on the go, these tips will streamline your routine and leave you with more time to enjoy your adventure, which is the whole point, after all!

Hack 35: Pre-Pack Toiletries in a Ready-to-Go Kit

✗ Time-Saving | ✈ Convenience

Save time before every trip by keeping a dedicated travel toiletries kit. Stock it with essentials, such as toothbrushes, toothpaste, and travel-sized liquids, and store in a TSA-approved bag. This will allow you to always make sure you're ready to pack and will completely eliminate the need to unpack your daily items.

Hack 36: Make a Packing List and Trim It Down

✗ Time-Saving | ⊠ Space-Saving

Before you even think about beginning to pack, write a checklist of everything you think you'll need. Then, cut the non-essentials in half. This process helps you focus on what's truly important, saves packing time, and prevents overpacking.

Hack 37: Place a Balloon Over Pump Bottles

Ⅹ Time-Saving | ✈ Convenience

Prevent spills in your toiletry bag by cutting the narrow end off a balloon and stretching it over the pump nozzle of your bottles. This simple hack keeps your packing mess-free and eliminates time wasted cleaning up leaks.

Hack 38: Pack Tops and Bottoms That Match

Ⅹ Time-Saving | ⊠ Space-Saving

Save time deciding what to wear by packing tops and bottoms that all coordinate with one another. This mix-and-match approach not only doubles your outfit options but also simplifies your morning routine.

Hack 39: Use a Poncho Instead of Multiple Items

Ⅹ Time-Saving | ⊠ Space-Saving | $ Money-Saving

Consider replacing a rain jacket, backpack cover, and umbrella with a single lightweight poncho. This multi-functional item keeps you dry while also reducing the number of things you need to pack.

Hack 40: Label Cables and Chargers Before Packing

Ⅹ Time-Saving | # Organizational

Use small tags or color-coded labels to identify your cables and chargers. This can really help save a ton of time when setting up your devices or digging through your bag to find the right one. It's especially helpful if you travel with multiple electronics.

Hack 41: Take Photos of Your Packed Bag for Reference

X Time-Saving | ✈ Convenience

Before zipping up your suitcase, snap a photo of its contents. If you need to repack during your trip or if your bag is inspected, the photo acts as a quick guide to save time and ensure nothing gets left behind. This photo will also help you to remember exactly how you packed, so that you can repeat packing in the same way, if necessary, and fit everything in for all legs of your trip.

Hack 42: Organize Travel Documents in a Single Folder

X Time-Saving | # Organizational

Keep all your travel documents—like your passport, boarding passes, and hotel confirmations—in one folder or a zippered pouch. This eliminates the hassle of searching for papers at check-ins or security. Bonus points for going digital and using an app like Google Drive, and doubling up with screenshots that are easily accessible in your phone's photo albums.

Each of these time-saving hacks will help you create a more efficient travel routine, giving you the freedom to spend your time where it matters most. Whether it's skipping long lines, reducing time spent packing and unpacking, or organizing your travel essentials for easy access, these strategies are about more than saving minutes—they're about making the entire experience smoother.

Thoughtful preparation is the key to unlocking a stress-free journey. With everything you need at your fingertips, you'll avoid last-minute scrambles, feel more confident, and create more opportunities to enjoy the best parts of traveling.

In the next chapter, we'll turn our focus to saving money, offering practical tips to help you cut costs without sacrificing comfort or convenience. Because traveling smart isn't just about time—it's about making the most of your budget, too.

Chapter 7:
Money-Saving Hacks

TRAVEL CAN UNDOUBTEDLY BE EXPENSIVE, but packing smart can help to avoid so many unnecessary costs from before packing all the way through to unpacking and repacking. The money-saving hacks presented in this chapter are provided to help you cut expenses on things like baggage fees, last-minute purchases, and overpriced travel essentials, leaving you more room in your budget for the experiences that truly matter (and that will stay with you for a lifetime).

Hack 43: Pack Multi-Purpose Products

$ Money-Saving | ☒ Space-Saving

Choose multi-functional items, such as shampoo bars that double as body wash, or a sarong that can serve as a towel, blanket, or scarf. This reduces the need to buy additional items at your destination, saving both money and space.

Hack 44: Bring Laundry Powder Sheets for Washing Clothes

$ Money-Saving | ☒ Space-Saving

Instead of feeling tempted to pack clothing for every day with the intention of returning home with a bag full of dirty clothes, take lightweight, water-soluble laundry powder sheets with you. These allow you to wash your clothes on the go, avoiding the cost of hotel laundry services or additional outfits. And, as an added bonus: they're eco-friendly and save on suitcase space.

Hack 45: Use a Diaper as a Hidden Stash for Valuables

$ Money-Saving | ✈ Convenience

Store cash, jewelry, or other valuables inside a clean diaper. Thieves are unlikely to search a diaper, giving you additional peace of mind and potentially saving you from costly losses.

Hack 46: Save on Currency Exchange with Travel Cards

$ Money-Saving | ✈ Convenience

Instead of exchanging currency and paying the inevitable fees, opt to use a no-fee travel credit or debit card. This will allow you to avoid high currency exchange fees or ATM charges. This can save you a significant amount of money, especially on long trips or in countries with unfavorable exchange rates, not to mention, if you are a frequent traveler, you can make use of any card balances on your next trip.

Hack 47: Bring a Reusable Shopping Bag

$ Money-Saving | ⊠ Space-Saving | ✈ Convenience

Take a reusable bag with you to avoid paying for disposable ones at stores, which is common in many different countries. These lightweight bags can also double up as beach bags, laundry totes, or additional carry-ons.

Hack 48: Pack a Universal Adapter Instead of Multiple Chargers

$ Money-Saving | ⊠ Space-Saving | ✈ Convenience

Rather than buying individual adapters or chargers for different countries, invest in a universal travel adapter. These compact devices work with multiple outlet types and often include USB ports. This allows you to charge multiple devices at once. It's a cost-effective, space-saving solution that's especially useful for international trips, and the investment will save a lot in the long-run as you visit more countries with different outlets.

Hack 49: Bring a Reusable Water Bottle to Skip Airport Prices

$ Money-Saving | ⊠ Space-Saving

Instead of buying pricey bottled water at the airport, be sure to take a reusable water bottle with you. Most airports have free refill stations, and many destinations offer clean drinking water, helping you save over the course of your trip. And don't forget to refill your bottle on the way out of the airport at your destination.

Hack 50: Download Offline Maps Instead of Buying Guides

$ Money-Saving | ✈ Convenience

Skip pricey guidebooks or printed maps, and instead download offline maps on your smartphone. Apps like Google Maps allow you to navigate without data charges, saving money and space. This also makes sure that, if you are without an internet connection for any length of time, you won't become lost or stranded.

Hack 51: Use Local Apps for Transportation Deals

$ Money-Saving | ✈ Convenience

When traveling, download local rideshare or public transportation apps to find discounts or promotions for getting around. This can mount up to save a great deal of money compared to taxis or private cars, and also gives you more insight into the city and the opportunity to see things you might otherwise have not had the chance to see.

Hack 52: Use Free Souvenirs as Travel Keepsakes
$ Money-Saving | ⊠ Space-Saving
Rather than buying expensive souvenirs, which can often be somewhat lacking when it comes to quality, collect free or inexpensive items, such as postcards, museum brochures, or maps. They make great mementos and don't take up much room in your luggage. They can also feel a lot more authentic and sentimental when looking back on trips and memorabilia.

These hacks prove that traveling frequently doesn't need to mean spending more. By packing thoughtfully and planning ahead, you can cut a huge amount of unnecessary costs and stretch your budget even further, giving you more of the moments that truly matter.

Up next: a Quick Reference Index to tie everything together and make your packing hacks even easier to use.

Quick Reference Index

WELCOME TO THE QUICK REFERENCE Index, which provides your ultimate guide to making the most of this book when you need to quickly find or revisit something. This section is designed to help you navigate the many different hacks shared in this guide, which are grouped into lists according to their key benefits.

Whether you're trying to pack smarter, save time, stay organized, keep your travels stress-free, or stick to a budget, this index allows you to quickly find the hacks that matter most to you. By cross-referencing hacks that serve multiple purposes, you can discover even more ways to enhance your travel routine.

How to Use This Index
1. Find Hacks by Category:
     - Looking to maximize space in your luggage? Jump to the ⊠ Space-Saving Hacks chapter (page 23).
     - Want to speed up your packing or daily routine? Check out the ⵝ Time-Saving Hacks chapter (page 35).
     - Need to keep your packing and travel essentials tidy? Head to # Organizational Hacks (page 27).
2. Use Page Numbers for Navigation:
     - Each hack includes a page number, so you can quickly find the more detailed explanation in the main chapters.
3. Cross-Reference Multi-Benefit Hacks:

- o Hacks that serve multiple purposes are listed in every relevant category. For example, a hack that saves space and money will appear in both ⊠ Space-Saving Hacks and $ Money-Saving Hacks sections.
4. Tailor Hacks to Your Travel Style:
   - o At the end of this index, you'll find a special "Best For" section that highlights hacks tailored to specific types of travelers, such as business professionals, families, or budget-conscious adventurers.

This index has been designed to make your experience with the book as seamless and practical as possible, and to encourage you to regularly revisit its pages so that you can truly make the most of every single trip. Whether you're flipping through it at home before you travel or referencing it on the go, the Quick Reference Index is here to ensure you're always packing and traveling like a pro.

⊠ *Space-Saving Hacks*

Organizational Hacks

✈ *Convenience Hacks*

⌛ *Time-Saving Hacks*

$ *Money-Saving Hacks*

5. Bring a Reusable Shopping Bag – p. 40
6. Pack a Universal Adapter Instead of Multiple Chargers – p. 40
7. Bring a Reusable Water Bottle to Skip Airport Prices – p. 41
8. Download Offline Maps Instead of Buying Guides – p. 41
9. Use Local Apps for Transportation Deals – p. 41
10. Use Free Souvenirs as Travel Keepsakes – p. 42

Best For: Tailored Hacks for Every Traveler

This section takes the guesswork out of finding those hacks that align with your unique travel style. Whether you're planning a business trip, a family vacation, or a quick weekend getaway, we've curated the most relevant hacks from the book to suit your needs.

Best For Adventure Travelers

- Wear Your Bulkiest Clothes on the Plane (⊠ Space-Saving | $ Money-Saving) – p. 24
- Use a Skipping Rope as a Makeshift Clothesline (✈ Convenience) – p. 33
- Use Vacuum-Seal Bags to Shrink Bulky Items (⊠ Space-Saving) – p. 23
- Trim Your Body Care Routine with Multi-Purpose Products (✈ Convenience | ⊠ Space-Saving) – p. 32
- Pack a Universal Adapter Instead of Multiple Chargers ($ Money-Saving | ⊠ Space-Saving | ✈ Convenience) – p. 40

Best For Budget Travelers

- Bring Laundry Powder Sheets for Washing Clothes ($ Money-Saving | ⊠ Space-Saving) – p. 39
- Download Offline Maps Instead of Buying Guides ($ Money-Saving | ✈ Convenience) – p. 41
- Save on Currency Exchange with Travel Cards ($ Money-Saving | ✈ Convenience) – p. 40
- Use Free Souvenirs as Travel Keepsakes ($ Money-Saving | ⊠ Space-Saving) – p. 42
- Use a Diaper as a Hidden Stash for Valuables ($ Money-Saving | ✈ Convenience) – p. 40

Best For Business Travelers

- Pre-Pack Toiletries in a Ready-to-Go Kit (⌧ Time-Saving) – p. 35
- Organize Travel Documents in a Single Folder (⌧ Time-Saving | # Organizational) – p. 37
- Use a Universal Adapter Instead of Multiple Chargers ($ Money-Saving | ⊠ Space-Saving | ✈ Convenience) – p. 40
- Use Local Apps for Transportation Deals ($ Money-Saving | ✈ Convenience) – p. 41
- Clip Carabiners to Your Bag for Extra Storage (✈ Convenience | ⊠ Space-Saving) – p. 33

Best For Families

- Use Sectioned Tupperware for Snacks or Meals (✈ Convenience | $ Money-Saving) – p. 33

- Bring a Reusable Shopping Bag ($ Money-Saving | ⊠ Space-Saving | ✈ Convenience) – p. 40
- Pack Complete Outfits Instead of Random Items (⏱ Time-Saving | # Organizational) – p. 20
- Separate Dirty Laundry with Packing Cubes (# Organizational | ⊠ Space-Saving) – p. 29
- Use Dryer Sheets in Luggage for Fresh Clothes (✈ Convenience) – p. 33

Best For Weekend Getaways

- Don't Skip Packing Cubes (⊠ Space-Saving | # Organizational) – p. 19
- Roll Clothes Instead of Folding (⊠ Space-Saving | ⏱ Time-Saving) – p. 19
- Pack Multi-Use Items (⊠ Space-Saving | $ Money-Saving | ✈ Convenience) – p. 21
- Spray Cotton Pads with Perfume (✈ Convenience | ⊠ Space-Saving) – p. 21
- Bring a Reusable Water Bottle to Skip Airport Prices ($ Money-Saving | ⊠ Space-Saving) – p. 41

Final Thoughts

CONGRATULATIONS, TRAVELER—YOU'VE REACHED THE end of this guide, and with it, you've gained a treasure trove of tips, tricks, and hacks to make your journeys lighter, smarter, and more enjoyable. My hope is that this book has empowered you to look at packing and travel through a fresh lens—one where simplicity meets functionality, and every step feels just that little bit smoother.

Whether you're gearing up for a weekend getaway or preparing for the trip of a lifetime, you now have the tools to pack with confidence, save time, and avoid some of the unnecessary stresses we have come to normalize when embarking on adventures! From clever organization strategies to budget-friendly hacks, the tips in these pages are designed to give you additional freedom to focus on what truly matters: the experiences waiting for you on the other side of the journey.

Remember, packing smart isn't just about what you bring with you—it's about the freedom you create by leaving the unnecessary behind. With every hack you put into practice, you'll find yourself feeling lighter, not just in your suitcase, but in your mindset, too. No more worrying about overstuffed bags or forgotten essentials. Instead, you'll have the confidence to tackle your travels head-on, knowing that you're prepared for anything.

One important thing to remember is that this guide is just that—a guide. At the end of the day, the best way to travel is any way that truly works for you and brings you joy. Take the hacks that resonate, adapt them to fit your unique needs, and don't be afraid to experiment. Travel is an ever-evolving experience, and with each trip, you'll discover what makes you feel the most comfortable, efficient, and joyful.

However your travels look from this point on, I want to thank you... Thank you for taking this journey with me. Writing this book has been such a labor of love, inspired by my own adventures and the lessons I've learned along the way, not to mention my lovely friend who needed a go-to reference with all hacks neatly organized in one place (Scyller, you inspired this whole idea). If even one hack from these pages helps you feel more prepared, more at ease, or simply more excited about traveling, then I'll consider it a success.

So, what's next? Perhaps a dream destination you've always wanted to visit, or a spontaneous weekend trip just to get away? Whatever it is, I hope this guide gives you the tools and inspiration to make it happen with a greater degree of ease. The world is waiting for you, traveler, and now you're ready to meet it with everything you need and nothing you don't.

Here's to stress-free packing, lighter luggage, and the endless joy of exploration. Bon voyage!

—ALEX WYLER

References

jeffandlaurenshow. (2024, October). Instagram. Retrieved November 24, 2024, from https://www.instagram.com/jeffandlaurenshow/

Gupta, K. (2024, June 2). How to pack light when you're only travelling with a carry-on. CN Traveller. https://www.cntraveller.com/article/how-to-pack-light

How to Pack Light for Traveling. (n.d.). Rei. Retrieved November 24, 2024, from https://www.rei.com/learn/expert-advice/traveling-light.html

www.ingramcontent.com/pod-product-compliance
Lightning Source LLC
Chambersburg PA
CBHW032131050726
47590CB00008B/3044